Shakespeare's
Romeo & Juliet

Story Summary
Worksheets and Tests

By Gary Ciesla, M.S.

**Meets Common Core Standards in Reading &
Writing for U.S. High School Students**

authorHOUSE®

Shakespeare's
Romeo & Juliet

Story Summary
Worksheets & Tests

AuthorHouse™
1663 Liberty Drive
Bloomington, IN 47403
www.authorhouse.com
Phone: 1-800-839-8640

Published by AuthorHouse   11/05/2012

ISBN: 978-1-4685-3213-5 (sc)

DEDICATION

This book is dedicated to Morgan, John, Ben, Cindy, Chyann, Alex, J.T., Andy, Barry, Rachael, Zach, Nick, Darren, Devante, Kayleene, and Christian—students I remember very well from my days teaching at the Chester Academy—and also to my assistant Maria Arias, who was a faithful ally during the year we worked together with these youngsters. Thanks for the wonderful memories.

AN INTRODUCTORY NOTE TO TEACHERS
ABOUT THE DEVELOPMENT OF THIS PROJECT

Special Education teachers often face the daunting task of teaching particularly challenging works of literature, such as *Romeo and Juliet*. To help them and their students with these works, I have developed a series of *Story Summary Worksheets & Tests* for several books and plays which are found on the required reading lists of many, if not most, school districts. I believe the *Story Summary Worksheets & Tests* I have written will be recognized as being very useful for teachers and students to use.

To demonstrate how my work might be helpful within a classroom, I will describe a collaborative effort between a teacher (who I will identify as J.I.) and me as we worked together to help her students understand *Romeo & Juliet*.

In February and March of 2012 I corresponded via email with J.I. She was presenting *Romeo & Juliet* to the students in her Special Education classes. I provided her with the worksheets and tests in this series, and I encouraged her to provide feedback to me about how the students responded to them, and what could be done to increase the usefulness of the worksheets within in the classroom.

In the course of our email correspondence, J.I. wrote:

"I will definitely give you feedback as I get it from my students. I'm sure they would love to be part of the process. I'm going to use the materials in both my self-contained sections as well as my integrated co-teaching class. I truly believe your material will make Shakespeare easier and a less stressful experience for the students. In my experience, my 9th graders are always panicked (probably intimidated) about starting the play, and the review materials will be easier to use than my review worksheets. Your work will make them more successful ...when they take the unit and final exams they will encounter (later) this year."

During the development and creation of the *Romeo & Juliet* worksheets, J.I. wrote to me on several occasions with helpful feedback, which I immediately incorporated, for the work was being thoroughly classroom-tested, and I knew that in the end it would be much improved because of the feedback.

At one point, J.I.'s students asked her to pass on a request to me. Here is what she wrote:

"I have some feedback for you- I'm finishing Act 3. I love the materials- however, both my students and I have one major request if it's not too late...The lines on the summary sheets are too short and would it be possible for them to be numbered? When I review with them- I do read the page and they fill in the blanks. I'll state the correct answer out loud and then project the answer onto the board. Almost every student in my self-contained classes as well as my regular ed. class has asked for these two items."

After incorporating these suggestions from J.I. and her students, I sent an updated version along to her as an attachment to an email. A bit later J.I. wrote in response:

"I just projected the Act 5 worksheet and showed some of my students. They really liked the changes. And they say 'Thank you!' "

An important part of the project's development was the writing of the five tests, one for each act of the play. Although J.I.'s Special Education students would need practice in writing essays, we both knew that giving them too many essays would put a great burden on them, as completing essay questions is a particularly difficult task for students with learning difficulties. As a result, I made sure to include several short-answer questions in each test. J.I. commented in one of her emails about the inclusion of the short-answer questions:

"...I liked that each test had the short answer questions. It gave us the ability to get deeper understanding from them, without the "torture" of the dreaded essay from their perspective."

Given the stringent educational requirements that have been put in place in order to help students meet the Common Core Standards, it was nevertheless necessary to include some essay questions. Two were developed for the test. The students' task in Essay #1 was to read a quote from Shakespeare's *Othello* and describe how the quote could apply to the characters in *Romeo and Juliet*. When I sent it along to J.I., she responded with the following comment:

"The quote looks great. It's an interesting connection using *Othello* and *Romeo & Juliet* like that. The quote is appropriate and can be used to describe several characters. I also like the layout you designed for the page.

It separates the quote and makes it easier to focus on it. Very clean design. Awesome job!"

As a former Special Education and Alternative Education teacher, I know that many Special Education and Alternative Education students are frequently absent, and often don't do their homework. I believe that the *Romeo & Juliet Story Summary Worksheets & Tests* can help teachers provide the essential story summary information to these students who are at risk of missing that essential information because of absence or lack of self-discipline. J.I. commented on the value and usefulness of the worksheets in one of her emails:

"It's been very valuable- especially with students who are absent and then don't read missed assignments."

Working closely with J.I. on this project enabled me to tailor the work to meet the needs of her students, and incorporating several of the revisions she and her students suggested has proved invaluable, resulting in the finished version of the *Romeo & Juliet Story Summary Worksheets & Tests*.

In one of our last email exchanges, J.I. sent me very nice note of thanks:

"Your work has really been helpful to my students, so I am very grateful."

If you, as a teacher, look over the *Romeo & Juliet Story Summary Worksheets & Tests* and find that it would be helpful to have similar materials for another literary work that you use in your classroom, please contact me at gary.ciesla@gmail.com. Maybe we could collaborate together to develop some quality educational materials for the benefit of your students!

Gary Ciesla
October 2012

Contents

"*For never was a story of more woe*

than this of Juliet and her Romeo."

-William Shakespeare, Romeo & Juliet

Suggestions for Using the Worksheets:

The fourteen *Romeo & Juliet Story Summary Worksheets & Tests* in this book have been written to help students understand the key points of this classic tale by William Shakespeare. Each two-page spread contains an answer key and a corresponding student page, and each worksheet covers a part of the play that can be read during a classroom period lasting approximately forty minutes.

The Story Summary worksheets can be used in several different ways:

- At the start of the class as a "Do Now" activity;
- As an in-class assignment after a section of the play has been read;
- As a homework assignment for students to complete;
- As a quiz to measure student understanding of the play;
- As a way to assist those students who are frequently absent from class;
- As a way for the teacher to quickly review specific sections of the play.

Every student worksheet contains twelve choices and usually twelve blanks, unless otherwise specified. Special notes are included on the bottom of those pages where alternate directions are necessary.

Appendix A includes five tests, one for each act of the play, along with the corresponding answer keys. Each test contains story ordering activities, as well as questions which require that the students write in full and complete sentences. Other types of questions, which differ from test to test, include character identification, multiple choice, true-false, and short-answer questions. In addition to the five tests, *Appendix A* also includes two essay questions.

Appendix B contains a list of the five Common Core Reading Standards for Literature that this edition of the *Romeo & Juliet Story Summary Worksheets & Tests* helps students meet.

The *Story Summary Worksheets* effectively and faithfully summarize the story of *Romeo & Juliet*. It is my hope that these *Story Summary Worksheets & Tests* will be useful for you and your students as you read this classic and timeless tale by William Shakespeare.

ACT 1, Scene 1   ANSWER KEY

The story of *Romeo and Juliet* opens in the city of (1) VERONA. Two families, the House of (2) CAPULET and the House of (3) MONTAGUE, have been fighting each other in the streets on several occasions, and the play opens with yet another quarrel. The fighting only stops when the (4) PRINCE OF VERONA issues a (5) DECREE saying that anyone who fights in the streets of the city will be (6) CONDEMNED TO DEATH.

Romeo, the (7) HEIR of the Montague clan, did not take part in any of the fighting. He has been very (8) SAD and hasn't told anyone what is troubling him. Romeo's parents ask his cousin (9) BENVOLIO to find out what is the matter with Romeo. The cousin learns that Romeo is in love with a young lady named (10) ROSALINE, but she doesn't love him. Benvolio tells Romeo that he should go out and (11) LOOK AT OTHER WOMEN to help cure his sadness.

Note: JULIET is purposely placed among the choices, but it is an incorrect answer.

DECREE	CAPULET	LOOK AT OTHER WOMEN
SAD	ROSALINE	PRINCE OF VERONA
MONTAGUE	HEIR	CONDEMNED TO DEATH
JULIET	BENVOLIO	VERONA

Student Name: _____   **ACT 1, Scene 1**

Directions: Fill in each blank using answers from the list at the bottom of the page.

The story of *Romeo and Juliet* opens in the city of (1) _____.
Two families, the House of (2) _____ and the House of
(3) _____, have been fighting each other in the streets on several
occasions, and the play opens with yet another quarrel. The fighting only stops when the
(4) _____ issues a (5) _____ saying that
anyone who fights in the streets of the city will be (6) _____.

Romeo, the (7) _____ of the Montague clan, did not take
part in any of the fighting. He has been very (8) _____ and hasn't
told anyone what is troubling him. Romeo's parents ask his cousin (9) _____
to find out what is the matter with Romeo. The cousin learns that Romeo is in love with
a young lady named (10) _____, but she doesn't love him.
Benvolio tells Romeo that he should go out and (11) _____ to
help cure his sadness.

DECREE	CAPULET	LOOK AT OTHER WOMEN
SAD	ROSALINE	PRINCE OF VERONA
MONTAGUE	HEIR	CONDEMNED TO DEATH
JULIET	BENVOLIO	VERONA

ACT 1, Scenes 2 & 3   ANSWER KEY

In scene two, Lord Capulet speaks with (1) PARIS, a young relative of the (2) PRINCE OF VERONA, who hopes to marry Lord Capulet's 14-year-old daughter (3) JULIET. Lord Capulet is planning a gala feast, and he invites Paris to attend and try to (4) WIN JULIET'S HEART. If Paris can do that, Lord Capulet will (5) AGREE TO THE MARRIAGE. Lord Capulet then gives a guest list to one of his servants with instructions to go out and personally invite all of the people on the list. Since the servant (6) CANNOT READ he looks for someone who can, and the first person he meets happens to be (7) ROMEO. Romeo reads the list and finds out that (8) ROSALINE, the woman he loves, will be at the feast.

In scene three, (9) LADY CAPULET learns that Paris has asked for Juliet's (10) HAND IN MARRIAGE. She wants to know if Juliet is (11) IN FAVOR OF THIS MATCH, and so Lady Capulet asks the (12) NURSE to bring Juliet to her. Lady Capulet then talks with Juliet and tells her that Paris will attend that evening's gala feast. Juliet says that she will see whether or not she likes him.

ROSALINE	ROMEO	WIN JULIET'S HEART
LADY CAPULET	PARIS	IN FAVOR OF THIS MATCH
PRINCE OF VERONA	NURSE	HAND IN MARRIAGE
CANNOT READ	JULIET	AGREE TO THE MARRIAGE

Student Name: _____   **ACT 1, Scenes 2 & 3**

| **Directions: Fill in each blank using answers from the list at the bottom of the page.** |

In scene two, Lord Capulet speaks with (1) _____, a young relative of the (2) _____, who hopes to marry Lord Capulet's 14-year-old daughter (3) _____. Lord Capulet is planning a gala feast, and he invites Paris to attend and try to (4) _____. If Paris can do that, Lord Capulet will (5) _____. Lord Capulet then gives a guest list to one of his servants with instructions to go out and personally invite all of the people on the list. Since the servant (6) _____ he looks for someone who can, and the first person he meets happens to be (7) _____. Romeo reads the list and finds out that (8) _____, the woman he loves, will be at the feast.

In scene three, (9) _____ learns that Paris has asked for Juliet's (10) _____. She wants to know if Juliet is (11) _____, and so Lady Capulet asks the (12) _____ to bring Juliet to her. Lady Capulet then talks with Juliet and tells her that Paris will attend that evening's gala feast. Juliet says that she will see whether or not she likes him.

ROSALINE	ROMEO	WIN JULIET'S HEART
LADY CAPULET	PARIS	IN FAVOR OF THIS MATCH
PRINCE OF VERONA	NURSE	HAND IN MARRIAGE
CANNOT READ	JULIET	AGREE TO THE MARRIAGE

ACT 1, Scenes 4 & 5   ANSWER KEY

Romeo, his cousin (1) BENVOLIO, and their friend (2) MERCUTIO are on their way to the gala feast being held at the home of Lord and Lady Capulet, where they will try to enter in disguise. Romeo says that he has a heavy heart and he only wants to carry the torch for the group. He also declares that he doesn't want to dance, for he is very sad about his unanswered love for (3) ROSALINE. His friends urge him to be rough with love and beat it down. Romeo also tells his friends of a (4) TROUBLING DREAM OF DEATH he has had, even as he urges his friends onward toward the Capulet residence.

Romeo and his friends arrive at the feast wearing (5) MASKS because they have not been invited, and also because they want to disguise their identity as (6) MONTAGUES, who are the enemies of the Capulets. Nevertheless, Lord Capulet welcomes them warmly, encouraging them to (7) DANCE. Romeo looks for Rosaline but then notices Juliet, and he immediately falls in love with her. When Romeo asks a servant what her name is, Lord Capulet's nephew (8) TYBALT, who is Romeo's (9) FIERCE ENEMY, overhears him speak and recognizes him. Tybalt wants to fight Romeo right then and there, but Lord Capulet prevents it. Romeo makes his way over to Juliet and charms her, and they exchange kisses. As Act One ends, both of these (10) STAR-CROSSED LOVERS discover that their families are (11) ENEMIES OF EACH OTHER.

Note: SING is purposely placed among the choices, but it is an incorrect answer.

MASKS	ROSALINE	STAR-CROSSED LOVERS
SING	TYBALT	TROUBLING DREAM OF DEATH
MERCUTIO	BENVOLIO	FIERCE ENEMY
MONTAGUES	DANCE	ENEMIES OF EACH OTHER

Student Name: _____   **ACT 1, Scenes 4 & 5**

| **Directions: Fill in each blank using answers from the list at the bottom of the page.** |

Romeo, his cousin (1) _____, and their friend (2) _____ are on their way to the gala feast being held at the home of Lord and Lady Capulet, where they will try to enter in disguise. Romeo says that he has a heavy heart and he only wants to carry the torch for the group. He also declares that he doesn't want to dance, for he is very sad about his unanswered love for (3) _____. His friends urge him to be rough with love and beat it down. Romeo also tells his friends of a (4) _____ he has had, even as he urges his friends onward toward the Capulet residence.

Romeo and his friends arrive at the feast wearing (5) _____ because they have not been invited, and also because they want to disguise their identity as (6) _____, who are the enemies of the Capulets. Nevertheless, Lord Capulet welcomes them warmly, encouraging them to (7) _____. Romeo looks for Rosaline but then notices Juliet, and he immediately falls in love with her. When Romeo asks a servant what her name is, Lord Capulet's nephew (8) _____, who is Romeo's (9) _____, overhears him speak and recognizes him. Tybalt wants to fight Romeo right then and there, but Lord Capulet prevents it. Romeo makes his way over to Juliet and charms her, and they exchange kisses. As Act One ends, both of these (10) _____ discover their families are (11) _____.

MASKS	ROSALINE	STAR-CROSSED LOVERS
SING	TYBALT	TROUBLING DREAM OF DEATH
MERCUTIO	BENVOLIO	FIERCE ENEMY
MONTAGUES	DANCE	ENEMIES OF EACH OTHER

ACT 2, Scenes 1 & 2   ANSWER KEY

Romeo leaves the house of the (1) CAPULETS at the end of the gala feast, but his heart remains there. As he walks down the lane that runs by the orchard wall beside Juliet's house, he realizes he cannot go any further away from her. He must (2) CLIMB THE WALL into the orchard. Romeo's friends (3) BENVOLIO and (4) MERCUTIO search for Romeo and call for him but go home once they realize that Romeo (5) DOES NOT WANT TO BE FOUND.

Juliet is unable to sleep and comes out onto the (6) BALCONY overlooking the orchard. She speaks, not knowing that Romeo is standing below the balcony listening. She says that he should deny his name of (7) MONTAGUE, or else she will deny her name of Capulet so that they can be together. When Romeo speaks, Juliet is startled, wondering how he managed to climb over the orchard wall. She also expresses (8) CONCERN FOR HIS SAFETY, knowing that if her family finds out that Romeo is on their property, they will try to (9) KILL HIM. The intensity of their passion and love for each other is such that Romeo says he will only be satisfied if they are able to (10) MARRY. Juliet says that in order to prove Romeo's honor and purpose for marrying her, she will send a (11) MESSENGER to him at 9 o'clock the next morning in order to find out where and when the wedding ceremony will be held. Romeo promises to go to see his friend (12) FRIAR LAURENCE in order to ask for the priest's help in this matter.

KILL HIM	MERCUTIO	FRIAR LAURENCE
BENVOLIO	MESSENGER	CLIMB THE WALL
MARRY	CAPULETS	CONCERN FOR HIS SAFETY
BALCONY	MONTAGUE	DOES NOT WANT TO BE FOUND

Student Name: _____ **ACT 2, Scenes 1 & 2**

| Directions: Fill in each blank using answers from the list at the bottom of the page. |

Romeo leaves the house of the (1) _____ at the end of the gala feast, but his heart remains there. As he walks down the lane that runs by the orchard wall beside Juliet's house, he realizes he cannot go any further away from her. He must (2) _____ into the orchard. Romeo's friends (3) _____ and (4) _____ search for Romeo and call for him but go home once they realize that Romeo (5) _____.

Juliet is unable to sleep and comes out onto the (6) _____ overlooking the orchard. She speaks, not knowing that Romeo is standing below the balcony listening. She says that he should deny his name of (7) _____, or else she will deny her name of Capulet so that they can be together. When Romeo speaks, Juliet is startled, wondering how he managed to climb over the orchard wall. She also expresses (8) _____, knowing that if her family finds out that Romeo is on their property, they will try to (9) _____. The intensity of their passion and love for each other is such that Romeo says he will only be satisfied if they are able to (10) _____. Juliet says that in order to prove Romeo's honor and purpose for marrying her, she will send a (11) _____ to him at 9 o'clock the next morning in order to find out where and when the wedding ceremony will be held. Romeo promises to go to see his friend (12) _____ in order to ask for the priest's help in this matter.

KILL HIM	MERCUTIO	FRIAR LAURENCE
BENVOLIO	MESSENGER	CLIMB THE WALL
MARRY	CAPULETS	CONCERN FOR HIS SAFETY
BALCONY	MONTAGUE	DOES NOT WANT TO BE FOUND

ACT 2, Scenes 3 & 4   ANSWER KEY

Romeo goes to the cell of his (1) FRIEND, an old priest named (2) FRIAR LAURENCE. The priest realizes that Romeo is very serious about his love for Juliet and agrees to perform a (3) SECRET WEDDING CEREMONY. The priest hopes the marriage will help the two warring families (4) FORGET THEIR HATRED toward each other so that they can (5) LIVE IN PEACE.

Benvolio and Mercutio spent time looking for Romeo. They went to his home, and there they found a letter from (6) TYBALT challenging Romeo (7) TO A DUEL. When Benvolio and Mercutio finally locate Romeo, they are very glad to see him (8) IN FINE SPIRITS once again. Juliet's nurse also finds Romeo, and she tells him of her opinions about (9) PARIS, and how sweet Juliet was when (10) SHE WAS A BABY. Romeo doesn't care to hear about any of that. He only wants to give the nurse a message for Juliet: Juliet should go to (11) FRIAR LAURENCE'S CELL that afternoon, for the priest has agreed to (12) PERFORM THE WEDDING CEREMONY.

PARIS	FRIAR LAURENCE	PERFORM THE WEDDING CEREMONY
LIVE IN PEACE	IN FINE SPIRITS	FRIAR LAURENCE'S CELL
FRIEND	TO A DUEL	SECRET WEDDING CEREMONY
TYBALT	SHE WAS A BABY	FORGET THEIR HATRED

Student Name: _____   **ACT 2, Scenes 3 & 4**

| Directions: Fill in each blank using answers from the list at the bottom of the page. |

Romeo goes to the cell of his (1) _____, an old priest named (2) _____. The priest realizes that Romeo is very serious about his love for Juliet and agrees to perform a (3) _____. The priest hopes the marriage will help the two warring families (4) _____ toward each other so that they can (5) _____.

Benvolio and Mercutio spent time looking for Romeo. They went to his home, and there they found a letter from (6) _____ challenging Romeo (7) _____. When Benvolio and Mercutio finally locate Romeo, they are very glad to see him (8) _____ once again. Juliet's nurse also finds Romeo, and she tells him of her opinions about (9) _____, and how sweet Juliet was when (10) _____. Romeo doesn't care to hear about any of that. He only wants to give the nurse a message for Juliet: Juliet should go to (11) _____ that afternoon, for the priest has agreed to (12) _____.

PARIS	FRIAR LAURENCE	PERFORM THE WEDDING CEREMONY
LIVE IN PEACE	IN FINE SPIRITS	FRIAR LAURENCE'S CELL
FRIEND	TO A DUEL	SECRET WEDDING CEREMONY
TYBALT	SHE WAS A BABY	FORGET THEIR HATRED

ACT 2, Scenes 5 & 6   ANSWER KEY

Juliet had sent her nurse to find (1) ROMEO and since then has been waiting expectantly for news and information about the man she loves. When the old nurse finally does return, she is (2) IN PAIN and (3) OUT OF BREATH, and wants to talk to Juliet about how her (4) OLD BONES ACHE. Juliet, of course, doesn't want to hear any of that; she just wants to hear (5) NEWS ABOUT ROMEO. The nurse delays telling Juliet the message that Romeo has sent, causing Juliet to become very impatient. The old lady finally asks Juliet if she has (6) PERMISSION from her parents to go to see the Catholic priest, (7) FRIAR LAURENCE, in order to go to (8) CONFESSION. When Juliet says that she has permission to go, the nurse tells her that Romeo will be (9) WAITING THERE TO MARRY HER. Furthermore, the nurse says that she has to go and get a (10) LADDER and put it by (11) JULIET'S BALCONY because, as she tells Juliet, Romeo will have to use it to climb up after dark to get to a "bird's nest," which is the window to Juliet's bedroom.

As Romeo waits with Friar Laurence for Juliet to arrive, he tells the priest he welcomes the time of extreme joy he and Juliet will have, even if it is short. As long as they are able to marry, Romeo feels that (12) DEATH CAN DO WHAT IT PLEASES. Act Two comes to an end once Juliet arrives and Friar Laurence performs the wedding ceremony, joining Romeo and Juliet in holy matrimony.

OUT OF BREATH	CONFESSION	DEATH CAN DO WHAT IT PLEASES
FRIAR LAURENCE	LADDER	OLD BONES ACHE
PERMISSION	ROMEO	NEWS ABOUT ROMEO
JULIET'S BALCONY	IN PAIN	WAITING THERE TO MARRY HER

Romeo & Juliet Story Summary Worksheets

Student Name: _____   **ACT 2, Scenes 5 & 6**

| Directions: Fill in each blank using answers from the list at the bottom of the page. |

Juliet had sent her nurse to find (1) _____ and since then has been waiting expectantly for news and information about the man she loves. When the old nurse finally does return, she is (2) _____ and (3) _____, and wants to talk to Juliet about how her (4) _____. Juliet, of course, doesn't want to hear any of that; she just wants to hear (5) _____. The nurse delays telling Juliet the message that Romeo has sent, causing Juliet to become very impatient. The old lady finally asks Juliet if she has (6) _____ from her parents to go to see the Catholic priest, (7) _____, in order to go to (8) _____. When Juliet says that she has permission to go, the nurse tells her that Romeo will be (9) _____. Furthermore, the nurse says that she has to go and get a (10) _____ and put it by (11) _____ because, as she tells Juliet, Romeo will have to use it to climb up after dark to get to a "bird's nest," which is the window to Juliet's bedroom.

As Romeo waits with Friar Laurence for Juliet to arrive, he tells the priest he welcomes the time of extreme joy he and Juliet will have, even if it is short. As long as they are able to marry, Romeo feels that (12) _____.
Act Two comes to an end once Juliet arrives and Friar Laurence performs the wedding ceremony, joining Romeo and Juliet in holy matrimony.

OUT OF BREATH	CONFESSION	DEATH CAN DO WHAT IT PLEASES
FRIAR LAURENCE	LADDER	OLD BONES ACHE
PERMISSION	ROMEO	NEWS ABOUT ROMEO
JULIET'S BALCONY	IN PAIN	WAITING THERE TO MARRY HER

13

ACT 3, Scene 1   ANSWER KEY

At the start of Act Three, Benvolio and Mercutio are walking about on a hot day in Verona's public square. Benvolio wants them both to go inside because hot weather leads to (1) QUARRELS, and Benvolio wants to avoid trouble with the (2) CAPULETS. Tybalt appears, looking for Romeo, wanting to challenge him to a duel. When Romeo enters the square, he tries to be (3) FRIENDLY towards Tybalt because Tybalt is Juliet's (4) FIRST COUSIN. Even though Tybalt taunts him, Romeo (5) REFUSES to draw his sword. However, this taunting makes (6) MERCUTIO angry, and he challenges Tybalt to a duel instead. Romeo tries to break up their fight and keep the peace. He even stands between the two (7) SWORDSMEN. But Tybalt's sword slips under Romeo's arm, (8) FATALLY WOUNDING Mercutio. Once Romeo sees that his friend Mercutio is dead, he becomes enraged and challenges Tybalt to a duel. Their swords clash and Tybalt is killed.

Romeo realizes what he has done as he stands over Tybalt's body. Not only has he killed Juliet's cousin, he has also doomed himself to death because of the (9) DECREE of the Prince of Verona. Benvolio convinces Romeo to go away quickly, and then does the best he can to explain to the (10) PRINCE OF VERONA, as well as to the elders of both the Montague and Capulet families, what happened in the fight. Benvolio's story does nothing to soften the heart of the Prince of Verona, and the prince declares that Romeo is to be (11) EXILED from Verona. Romeo must leave Verona by (12) DAYBREAK and never return to the city again.

FRIENDLY	MERCUTIO	PRINCE OF VERONA
DECREE	QUARRELS	FATALLY WOUNDING
REFUSES	EXILED	FIRST COUSIN
CAPULETS	DAYBREAK	SWORDSMEN

Student Name: _____   **ACT 3, Scene 1**

Directions: Fill in each blank using answers from the list at the bottom of the page.

At the start of Act Three, Benvolio and Mercutio are walking about on a hot day in Verona's public square. Benvolio wants them both to go inside because hot weather leads to (1) _____, and Benvolio wants to avoid trouble with the (2) _____. Tybalt appears, looking for Romeo, wanting to challenge him to a duel. When Romeo enters the square, he tries to be (3) _____ towards Tybalt because Tybalt is Juliet's (4) _____. Even though Tybalt taunts him, Romeo (5) _____ to draw his sword. However, this taunting makes (6) _____ angry, and he challenges Tybalt to a duel instead. Romeo tries to break up their fight and keep the peace. He even stands between the two (7) _____. But Tybalt's sword slips under Romeo's arm, (8) _____ Mercutio. Once Romeo sees that his friend Mercutio is dead, he becomes enraged and challenges Tybalt to a duel. Their swords clash and Tybalt is killed.

Romeo realizes what he has done as he stands over Tybalt's body. Not only has he killed Juliet's cousin, he has also doomed himself to death because of the (9) _____ of the Prince of Verona. Benvolio convinces Romeo to go away quickly, and then does the best he can to explain to the (10) _____, as well as to the elders of both the Montague and Capulet families, what happened in the fight. Benvolio's story does nothing to soften the heart of the Prince of Verona, and the prince declares that Romeo is to be (11) _____ from Verona. Romeo must leave Verona by (12) _____ and never return to the city again.

FRIENDLY	MERCUTIO	PRINCE OF VERONA
DECREE	QUARRELS	FATALLY WOUNDING
REFUSES	EXILED	FIRST COUSIN
CAPULETS	DAYBREAK	SWORDSMEN

ACT 3, Scenes 2 & 3   ANSWER KEY

Juliet is excited as she waits for Romeo. (1) HER NURSE arrives and brings her the news that Romeo has killed Tybalt and has been banished from Verona forever. Juliet is beside herself with grief over the matter, but comforts herself by reasoning that Tybalt would have killed Romeo if he could have. Still she fears she will never again (2) SEE ROMEO, but her nurse comforts her by saying she knows that Romeo is (3) HIDING in (4) FRIAR LAURENCE'S CELL. The nurse will go to him and send him to Juliet this evening. Juliet gives her (5) A RING to take to Romeo.

Friar Laurence has told Romeo that the Prince of Verona has issued an order that Romeo is to be banished from the city forever. To Romeo, this is worse than a (6) DEATH SENTENCE, for if he is banished he will (7) NEVER SEE JULIET AGAIN. He also fears that Juliet will think of him as a (8) MURDERER. When the nurse arrives, she tells Romeo that Juliet is weeping and just as upset as he is. Friar Laurence tells Romeo that he should stop crying and act more like a man. The Friar suggests that Romeo should go to Juliet later that night to comfort her, but then flee to (9) MANTUA and live there until the time when the priest can (10) ANNOUNCE THE MARRIAGE of these two lovers, beg the (11) PARDON OF THE PRINCE, and then bring Romeo back to Verona. The nurse says that she will go and tell Juliet that Romeo will come to her later that night. She gives Romeo the ring that Juliet gave to her. Friar Laurence advises Romeo to be careful to either leave Verona while it is still night, or leave at the break of day dressed in a (12) DISGUISE.

HIDING	A RING	ANNOUNCE THE MARRIAGE
DISGUISE	DEATH SENTENCE	PARDON OF THE PRINCE
MANTUA	HER NURSE	FRIAR LAURENCE'S CELL
MURDERER	SEE ROMEO	NEVER SEE JULIET AGAIN

Student Name: _____   **ACT 3, Scenes 2 & 3**

Directions: Fill in each blank using answers from the list at the bottom of the page.

Juliet is excited as she waits for Romeo. (1) _____ arrives and brings her the news that Romeo has killed Tybalt and has been banished from Verona forever. Juliet is beside herself with grief over the matter, but comforts herself by reasoning that Tybalt would have killed Romeo if he could have. Still she fears she will never again (2) _____, but her nurse comforts her by saying she knows that Romeo is (3) _____ in (4) _____. The nurse will go to him and send him to Juliet this evening. Juliet gives her (5) _____ to take to Romeo.

Friar Laurence has told Romeo that the Prince of Verona has issued an order that Romeo is to be banished from the city forever. To Romeo, this is worse than a (6) _____, for if he is banished he will (7) _____. He also fears that Juliet will think of him as a (8) _____. When the nurse arrives, she tells Romeo that Juliet is weeping and just as upset as he is. Friar Laurence tells Romeo that he should stop crying and act more like a man. The Friar suggests that Romeo should go to Juliet later that night to comfort her, but then flee to (9) _____ and live there until the time when the priest can (10) _____ of these two lovers, beg the (11) _____, and then bring Romeo back to Verona. The nurse says that she will go and tell Juliet that Romeo will come to her later that night. She gives Romeo the ring that Juliet gave to her. Friar Laurence advises Romeo to be careful to either leave Verona while it is still night, or leave at the break of day dressed in a (12) _____.

HIDING	A RING	ANNOUNCE THE MARRIAGE
DISGUISE	DEATH SENTENCE	PARDON OF THE PRINCE
MANTUA	HER NURSE	FRIAR LAURENCE'S CELL
MURDERER	SEE ROMEO	NEVER SEE JULIET AGAIN

ACT 3, Scenes 4 & 5   ANSWER KEY

Lord and Lady Capulet meet with Paris and make plans for the young man to marry Juliet in three days. During the conversation, Lord Capulet boasts of his daughter's (1) OBEDIENCE to him, and he sends Lady Capulet to inform Juliet about the upcoming wedding arrangement.

Romeo and Juliet are just saying their goodbyes to one another as the morning light is beginning to brighten the eastern sky. Juliet's nurse arrives to tell Juliet that her mother is coming to her chamber. Romeo and Juliet share one last kiss before he leaves for (2) MANTUA.

When Juliet's mother enters and sees her daughter's sadness, she assumes Juliet is (3) STILL GRIEVING over the death of her cousin Tybalt. She tells Juliet that someone will give Romeo (4) A POISONED DRINK in Mantua in order to get revenge against him. She also talks to Juliet about the wedding plans that have been made for her, but Juliet stuns her by saying that she intends to marry Romeo. When Juliet's father enters the chamber, she tells him that she is thankful he tried to find her a good husband, but she is not proud of the arrangement and hates the idea of it. Upon hearing this, Lord Capulet explodes in anger toward his daughter. He says that if Juliet doesn't go to the church on Thursday, (5) HE WILL DRAG HER THERE on a cart. When the nurse tries to speak in Juliet's defense, he tells her to be quiet and then calls her a (6) MUMBLING FOOL. Juliet's father threatens to (7) PUT HIS DAUGHTER OUT of the house to hang, beg, starve, or even die in the streets. He declares that (8) HE WILL DISOWN HER if she does not marry Paris. Juliet begs her mother to (9) DELAY THE MARRIAGE for a month, or a week, but her mother will not listen to her. When Juliet appeals to her nurse, she says that her husband is on earth, and her vow is recorded in heaven, and Juliet says (10) SHE CANNOT REMARRY unless her (11) HUSBAND DIES. Sadly, the nurse proclaims that Juliet will be better off if she (12) MARRIES PARIS. Finally, Juliet says that she is going to see Friar Laurence. As Act Three comes to an end, Juliet declares that if Friar Laurence cannot help her in this matter, she has the power to take her own life.

MANTUA	DELAY THE MARRIAGE	PUT HIS DAUGHTER OUT
HUSBAND DIES	A POISONED DRINK	SHE CANNOT REMARRY
MUMBLING FOOL	MARRIES PARIS	HE WILL DRAG HER THERE
OBEDIENCE	STILL GRIEVING	HE WILL DISOWN HER

Student Name: _____   **ACT 3, Scenes 4 & 5**

Directions: Fill in each blank using answers from the list at the bottom of the page.

Lord and Lady Capulet meet with Paris and make plans for the young man to marry Juliet in three days. During the conversation, Lord Capulet boasts of his daughter's (1) _____ to him, and he sends Lady Capulet to inform Juliet about the upcoming wedding arrangement.

Romeo and Juliet are just saying their goodbyes to one another as the morning light is beginning to brighten the eastern sky. Juliet's nurse arrives to tell Juliet that her mother is coming to her chamber. Romeo and Juliet share one last kiss before he leaves for (2) _____ .

When Juliet's mother enters and sees her daughter's sadness, she assumes Juliet is (3) _____ over the death of her cousin Tybalt. She tells Juliet that someone will give Romeo (4) _____ in Mantua in order to get revenge against him. She also talks to Juliet about the wedding plans that have been made for her, but Juliet stuns her by saying that she intends to marry Romeo. When Juliet's father enters the chamber, she tells him that she is thankful he tried to find her a good husband, but she is not proud of the arrangement and hates the idea of it. Upon hearing this, Lord Capulet explodes in anger toward his daughter. He says that if Juliet doesn't go to the church on Thursday, (5) _____ on a cart. When the nurse tries to speak in Juliet's defense, he tells her to be quiet and then calls her a (6) _____ . Juliet's father threatens to (7) _____ of the house to hang, beg, starve, or even die in the streets. He declares that (8) _____ if she does not marry Paris. Juliet begs her mother to (9) _____ for a month, or a week, but her mother will not listen to her. When Juliet appeals to her nurse, Juliet says that her husband is on earth, and her vow is recorded in heaven, and Juliet says (10) _____ unless her (11) _____ . Sadly, the nurse proclaims that Juliet will be better off if she (12) _____ . Finally, Juliet says that she is going to see Friar Laurence. As Act Three comes to an end, Juliet declares that if Friar Laurence cannot help her in this matter, she has the power to take her own life.

MANTUA	DELAY THE MARRIAGE	PUT HIS DAUGHTER OUT
HUSBAND DIES	A POISONED DRINK	SHE CANNOT REMARRY
MUMBLING FOOL	MARRIES PARIS	HE WILL DRAG HER THERE
OBEDIENCE	STILL GRIEVING	HE WILL DISOWN HER

ACT 4, Scenes 1, 2 & 3   ANSWER KEY

Paris has gone to see Friar Laurence in order to speak about the wedding plans. The priest knows of course, that Juliet is married to Romeo, but he is unable to say that. He talks to Paris about (1) DELAYING THE WEDDING. Juliet arrives and has a difficult conversation with Paris. He speaks as if he will own her as his wife after the wedding ceremony on Thursday, and she is as cold as she can be toward him. When Juliet asks Friar Laurence if she should come back another time to speak to him, the priest asks Paris to leave so that he may speak privately to Juliet.

Juliet asks Friar Laurence for his help but says that if he can't help her, she is fully ready to (2) TAKE HER OWN LIFE. She states that her husband is Romeo, and she cannot (3) MARRY PARIS. Friar Laurence then tells her of a plan he has to help her (4) FAKE HER DEATH so that the wedding ceremony will not take place. He tells Juliet to go to her home and make certain that she is (5) COMPLETELY ALONE the night before the wedding is scheduled. During that night, he says that Juliet is to (6) DRINK A POTION that will cause her to fall into a (7) DEATH-LIKE SLEEP for forty-two hours. The priest says that she will be carried to the (8) FAMILY BURIAL VAULT in a coffin, where she will lie for the customary period of mourning. During that time, the priest says, he will send a (9) LETTER TO ROMEO, who will return from (10) MANTUA and take her back with him to that city once she awakens. She agrees to this plan.

When Juliet returns home, her father is very pleased that she now appears willing to go forward with the wedding plans to marry Paris. When Juliet goes to her bedroom, she asks the nurse to leave her alone for the night. Once she is alone, Juliet begins to worry that the secret potion (11) WILL NOT WORK, or that it will actually kill her, or that she will be buried alive in the vault before Romeo comes to rescue her. Juliet begins to go mad and thinks she sees the ghost of (12) TYBALT trying to find and kill Romeo. As the scene ends, Juliet drinks the secret potion and falls back upon her bed.

TYBALT	DRINK A POTION	LETTER TO ROMEO
WILL NOT WORK	TAKE HER OWN LIFE	DELAYING THE WEDDING
MARRY PARIS	DEATH-LIKE SLEEP	FAMILY BURIAL VAULT
MANTUA	FAKE HER DEATH	COMPLETELY ALONE

Student Name: _____ **ACT 4, Scenes 1, 2 & 3**

Directions: Fill in each blank using answers from the list at the bottom of the page.

Paris has gone to see Friar Laurence in order to speak about the wedding plans. The priest knows of course, that Juliet is married to Romeo, but he is unable to say that. He talks to Paris about (1) _____. Juliet arrives and has a difficult conversation with Paris. He speaks as if he will own her as his wife after the wedding ceremony on Thursday, and she is as cold as she can be toward him. When Juliet asks Friar Laurence if she should come back another time to speak to him, the priest asks Paris to leave so that he may speak privately to Juliet.

Juliet asks Friar Laurence for his help but says that if he can't help her, she is fully ready to (2) _____. She states that her husband is Romeo, and she cannot (3) _____. Friar Laurence then tells her of a plan he has to help her (4) _____ so that the wedding ceremony will not take place. He tells Juliet to go to her home, and make certain that she is (5) _____ the night before the wedding is scheduled. During that night, he says that Juliet is to (6) _____ that will cause her to fall into a (7) _____ for forty-two hours. The priest says that she will be carried to the (8) _____ in a coffin, where she will lie for the customary period of mourning. During that time, the priest says, he will send a (9) _____, who will return from (10) _____ and take her back with him to that city once she awakens. She agrees to this plan.

When Juliet returns home, her father is very pleased that she now appears willing to go forward with the wedding plans to marry Paris. When Juliet goes to her bedroom, she asks the nurse to leave her alone for the night. Once she is alone, Juliet begins to worry that the secret potion (11) _____, or that it will actually kill her, or that she will be buried alive in the vault before Romeo comes to rescue her. Juliet begins to go mad and thinks she sees the ghost of (12) _____ trying to find and kill Romeo. As the scene ends, Juliet drinks the secret potion and falls back upon her bed.

TYBALT	DRINK A POTION	LETTER TO ROMEO
WILL NOT WORK	TAKE HER OWN LIFE	DELAYING THE WEDDING
MARRY PARIS	DEATH-LIKE SLEEP	FAMILY BURIAL VAULT
MANTUA	FAKE HER DEATH	COMPLETELY ALONE

ACT 4, Scenes 4 & 5   ANSWER KEY

Since early on the morning of what was supposed to be (1) JULIET'S WEDDING DAY, her mother and father had been working, (2) PREPARING FOR THE WEDDING. Servants are bringing in supplies for the feast, and Juliet's father is directing them. Paris arrives, bringing with him a (3) BAND OF MUSICIANS, just as he had promised Lord Capulet. Juliet's father summons the nurse and tells her to go and (4) AWAKEN JULIET.

The nurse finds Juliet (5) "DEAD" on her bed, still dressed in her clothing, though we, as the audience, know that Juliet is just (6) SLEEPING. Lady and Lord Capulet enter and weep over Juliet's "dead" body. Friar Laurence and Paris come to Juliet's bedroom chamber, as they want to know if Juliet is ready to go to the church. Lord Capulet breaks the sad news to Paris that Juliet is "dead." Lady Capulet, the nurse, Paris, and Lord Capulet all share their sorrows over the "death" of Juliet. Friar Laurence pretends to offer (7) WORDS OF COMFORT to those who are mourning, saying that (8) HEAVEN has her now that she is no longer (9) "ALIVE."

Lord Capulet instructs his servants that all the things being prepared for Juliet's wedding are to be used for her (10) FUNERAL. Friar Laurence then suggests that Lord Capulet, Lady Capulet, and Paris go with him to the (11) GRAVE where they will place Juliet's body. The musicians, who were hired to play music for Juliet's wedding, (12) ARGUE over what kind of music they should play for her funeral as Act Four ends.

ALIVE	SLEEPING	BAND OF MUSICIANS
GRAVE	AWAKEN JULIET	WORDS OF COMFORT
HEAVEN	ARGUE	PREPARING FOR THE WEDDING
DEAD	FUNERAL	JULIET'S WEDDING DAY

Student Name: _____   **ACT 4, Scenes 4 & 5**

> **Directions: Fill in each blank using answers from the list at the bottom of the page.**

Since early on the morning of what was supposed to be (1) _____,
her mother and father had been working, (2) _____. Servants are
bringing in supplies for the feast, and Juliet's father is directing them. Paris arrives,
bringing with him a (3) _____, just as he had promised Lord
Capulet. Juliet's father summons the nurse and tells her to go and (4) _____.

The nurse finds Juliet (5) "_____" on her bed, still dressed in her
clothing, though we, as the audience, know that Juliet is just (6) _____.
Lady and Lord Capulet enter and weep over Juliet's "dead" body. Friar Laurence and
Paris come to Juliet's bedroom chamber, as they want to know if Juliet is ready to go to
the church. Lord Capulet breaks the sad news to Paris that Juliet is "dead." Lady
Capulet, the nurse, Paris, and Lord Capulet all share their sorrows over the "death" of
Juliet. Friar Laurence pretends to offer (7) _____ to those
who are mourning, saying that (8) _____ has her now that she is no
longer (9) "_____."

Lord Capulet instructs his servants that all the things being prepared for Juliet's
wedding are to be used for her (10) _____. Friar Laurence then
suggests that Lord Capulet, Lady Capulet, and Paris go with him to the
(11) _____ where they will place Juliet's body. The musicians,
who were hired to play music for Juliet's wedding, (12) _____

ALIVE	SLEEPING	BAND OF MUSICIANS
GRAVE	AWAKEN JULIET	WORDS OF COMFORT
HEAVEN	ARGUE	PREPARING FOR THE WEDDING
DEAD	FUNERAL	JULIET'S WEDDING DAY

ACT 5, Scenes 1 & 2   ANSWER KEY

Romeo is in (1) MANTUA and in good spirits, thinking of Juliet and talking to himself about a dream he had concerning (2) HIS DEAR WIFE. In the dream, Juliet found him dead, but then she breathed life back into his body with (3) HER KISSES. Once revived, Romeo was surprised to find he had become (4) A KING.

As Romeo remembers this dream, his servant Balthasar arrives from Verona. He tells Romeo that Juliet is dead, and that her body now lies in the Capulet tomb. Upon hearing this, Romeo becomes very distraught and wonders how he can get his hands on (5) POISON so he can take his own life. He remembers that there is an apothecary - a drug store - nearby. Romeo goes there and arranges to buy a vial of poison from the owner, who is a very poor man. The owner sells it to him even though selling the poison is against the law, because he is desperate for Romeo's (6) GOLD. Once Romeo has the poison, he starts out on the road to Verona, heading to the tomb where Juliet's body lies.

Friar Laurence had written a letter to Romeo, just as he had promised, and asked his friend (7) FRIAR JOHN to personally deliver it as he was traveling to Mantua. The Friar intended to deliver the letter, but Verona city officials detained him inside a house where he was visiting. The officials were trying to control the outbreak of a deadly plague, and they feared that the house was (8) INFECTED WITH THAT PLAGUE. As a result, they would not let Friar John leave the house. Thus, he was kept from (9) DELIVERING THE LETTER to Romeo. Friar Laurence sensed this could be very dangerous, and realized that he must hurry as quickly as possible to get to the vault where Juliet slept, for it was important for him to be by her side (10) WHEN SHE AWOKE. He would then bring Juliet (11) TO HIS CELL and keep her there until he could successfully (12) CONTACT ROMEO.

POISON	TO HIS CELL	DELIVERING THE LETTER
FRIAR JOHN	HIS DEAR WIFE	WHEN SHE AWOKE
MANTUA	GOLD	CONTACT ROMEO
HER KISSES	A KING	INFECTED WITH THAT PLAGUE

24

Student Name: _____   **ACT 5, Scenes 1 & 2**

Directions: Fill in each blank using answers from the list at the bottom of the page.

Romeo is in (1) _____ and in good spirits, thinking of Juliet and talking to himself about a dream he had concerning (2) _____. In the dream, Juliet found him dead, but then she breathed life back into his body with (3) _____. Once revived, Romeo was surprised to find he had become (4) _____.

As Romeo remembers this dream, his servant Balthasar arrives from Verona. He tells Romeo that Juliet is dead, and that her body now lies in the Capulet tomb. Upon hearing this, Romeo becomes very distraught and wonders how he can get his hands on (5) _____ so he can take his own life. He remembers that there is an apothecary - a drug store - nearby. Romeo goes there and arranges to buy a vial of poison from the owner, who is a very poor man. The owner sells it to him even though selling the poison is against the law, because he is desperate for Romeo's (6) _____. Once Romeo has the poison, he starts out on the road to Verona, heading to the tomb where Juliet's body lies.

Friar Laurence had written a letter to Romeo, just as he had promised, and asked his friend (7) _____ to personally deliver it as he was traveling to Mantua. The Friar intended to deliver the letter, but Verona city officials detained him inside a house where he was visiting. The officials were trying to control the outbreak of a deadly plague, and they feared that the house was (8) _____. As a result, they would not let Friar John leave the house. Thus, he was kept from (9) _____ to Romeo. Friar Laurence sensed this could be very dangerous, and realized that he must hurry as quickly as possible to get to the vault where Juliet slept, for it was important for him to be by her side (10) _____. He would then bring Juliet (11) _____ and keep her there until he could successfully (12) _____.

POISON	TO HIS CELL	DELIVERING THE LETTER
FRIAR JOHN	HIS DEAR WIFE	WHEN SHE AWOKE
MANTUA	GOLD	CONTACT ROMEO
HER KISSES	A KING	INFECTED WITH THAT PLAGUE

ACT 5, Scene 3, Part A   ANSWER KEY

Paris and his servant arrive at Juliet's grave. He tells the servant to stand guard and (1) WHISTLE if anyone approaches. It isn't long before Paris hears the servant's whistle, and he hides so he can discreetly observe who has entered the courtyard. It is (2) ROMEO who has arrived, along with his servant Balthasar. Romeo tells Balthasar that he has (3) WRITTEN A LETTER to his father, Lord Montague, and he wants Balthasar to deliver it. He also gives Balthasar stern instructions to leave him alone and not interrupt him. Romeo lies by saying that he must take a (4) PRECIOUS RING from Juliet's finger and wants to be sure that he is (5) ALONE with her when he does it. Romeo then threatens Balthasar, saying that he will tear him limb from limb if he returns and interrupts. Once Balthasar leaves, Romeo pries open (6) JULIET'S TOMB. But then Paris steps forward from where he has been hiding and confronts Romeo, for Paris thinks Romeo has come to (7) DISHONOR THE DEAD bodies of Tybalt and Juliet. Paris tries to (8) ARREST him. Romeo warns Paris to leave him alone, but Paris continues to provoke him, and so they fight. During the duel Romeo stabs Paris, mortally wounding him. As Paris is dying, he asks Romeo to (9) HONOR his last request and place his body beside that of Juliet. Romeo honors this request and lays Paris in the tomb just as he had asked. Then, in a final act of desperation, Romeo speaks to Juliet, saying he will (10) LOOK UPON HER one last time and embrace her. He then (11) DRINKS THE POISON, steals (12) ONE LAST KISS from her lips, and dies.

ALONE	PRECIOUS RING	HONOR
WHISTLE	WRITTEN A LETTER	JULIET'S TOMB
ARREST	LOOK UPON HER	DISHONOR THE DEAD
ROMEO	ONE LAST KISS	DRINKS THE POISON

Student Name: _____ **ACT 5, Scene 3, Part A**

Directions: Fill in each blank using answers from the list at the bottom of the page.

Paris and his servant arrive at Juliet's grave. He tells the servant to stand guard and (1) _____ if anyone approaches. It isn't long before Paris hears the servant's whistle, and he hides so he can discreetly observe who has entered the courtyard. It is (2) _____ who has arrived, along with his servant Balthasar. Romeo tells Balthasar that he has (3) _____ to his father, Lord Montague, and he wants Balthasar to deliver it. He also gives Balthasar stern instructions to leave him alone and not interrupt him. Romeo lies by saying that he must take a (4) _____ from Juliet's finger and wants to be sure that he is (5) _____ with her when he does it. Romeo then threatens Balthasar, saying that he will tear him limb from limb if he returns and interrupts. Once Balthasar leaves, Romeo pries open (6) _____. But then Paris steps forward from where he has been hiding and confronts Romeo, for Paris thinks Romeo has come to (7) _____ bodies of Tybalt and Juliet. Paris tries to (8) _____ him. Romeo warns Paris to leave him alone, but Paris continues to provoke him, and so they fight. During the duel Romeo stabs Paris, mortally wounding him. As Paris is dying, he asks Romeo to (9) _____ his last request and place his body beside that of Juliet. Romeo honors this request and lays Paris in the tomb just as he had asked. Then, in a final act of desperation, Romeo speaks to Juliet, saying he will (10) _____ one last time and embrace her. He

_____ (11) _____, _____ (12) _____ _____ _____

lips, and dies.

ALONE	PRECIOUS RING	HONOR
WHISTLE	WRITTEN A LETTER	JULIET'S TOMB
ARREST	LOOK UPON HER	DISHONOR THE DEAD
ROMEO	ONE LAST KISS	DRINKS THE POISON

ACT 5, Scene 3, Part B   ANSWER KEY

When Friar Laurence enters the graveyard, he meets Romeo's servant (1) BALTHASAR. The servant had disobeyed Romeo's order and not left on his errand. Balthasar tells Friar Laurence that Romeo has been in the burial vault for at least half an hour. When the Friar enters the tomb, he sees that both Romeo and Paris are dead and he notices that Juliet is (2) BEGINNING TO AWAKEN. When Juliet is fully awake, she asks about her husband Romeo. Friar Laurence breaks the news to her that both Romeo and Paris are dead. He advises her to (3) LEAVE THE VAULT quickly as watchmen will soon arrive, but Juliet says she will stay. She even orders Friar Laurence to leave, which he does. Once alone, Juliet sees that Romeo poisoned himself, and she laments that there is no poison left that she can drink. When she hears the sounds of the watchmen approaching, she grabs Romeo's dagger, (4) STABS HERSELF, and falls upon his body. When the chief watchman enters the tomb and sees this horrible sight, he sends men to (5) NOTIFY THE PRINCE of Verona, the Capulets, and the Montagues. Others are ordered to (6) SEARCH THE GROUNDS, and they soon return with Romeo's servant Balthasar, and with Friar Laurence. The Prince of Verona and Lord and Lady Capulet soon arrive. When Lord Montague arrives, he brings the sad news that his wife (7) DIED earlier that evening. He says her death was caused by (8) GRIEF OVER ROMEO'S EXILE to Mantua.

Friar Laurence explains to the Prince of Verona and all assembled that he secretly married Romeo and Juliet on the day of Tybalt's death. He also admits he gave Juliet a sleeping potion that would give her a death-like appearance. The Friar says that he was there with Juliet when she awoke but left her alone in the tomb, where she took her own life. Paris' servant says that his master came to (9) LAY FLOWERS on Juliet's grave, and that he saw him (10) DRAW HIS SWORD on someone who was trying to enter Juliet's tomb. Balthasar, Romeo's servant, gives the Prince the letter he was supposed to deliver to Romeo's father. The Prince reads the letter and states that it confirms all of the facts that have been put forth in this matter.

As the play ends, Lord Capulet and Montague shake hands and offer their friendship to one another, with each of the men pledging to build beautiful (11) STATUES OF ROMEO AND JULIET to honor their memories. But the men both realize it was each family's (12) HATRED FOR THE OTHER that brought about the death of their children.

LAY FLOWERS	SEARCH THE GROUNDS	HATRED FOR THE OTHER
BALTHASAR	NOTIFY THE PRINCE	GRIEF OVER ROMEO'S EXILE
DRAW HIS SWORD	STABS HERSELF	BEGINNING TO AWAKEN
DIED	LEAVE THE VAULT	STATUES OF ROMEO AND JULIET

Student Name: _____ **ACT 5, Scene 3, Part B**

Directions: Fill in each blank using answers from the list at the bottom of the page.

When Friar Laurence enters the graveyard, he meets Romeo's servant (1) _____. The servant had disobeyed Romeo's order and not left on his errand. Balthasar tells Friar Laurence that Romeo has been in the burial vault for at least half an hour. When the Friar enters the tomb, he sees that both Romeo and Paris are dead and he notices that Juliet is (2) _____. When Juliet is fully awake, she asks about her husband Romeo. Friar Laurence breaks the news to her that both Romeo and Paris are dead. He advises her to (3) _____ quickly as watchmen will soon arrive, but Juliet says she will stay. She even orders Friar Laurence to leave, which he does. Once alone, Juliet sees that Romeo poisoned himself, and she laments that there is no poison left that she can drink. When she hears the sounds of the watchmen approaching, she grabs Romeo's dagger, (4) _____, and falls upon his body. When the chief watchman enters the tomb and sees this horrible sight, he sends men to (5) _____ of Verona, the Capulets, and the Montagues. Others are ordered to (6) _____, and they soon return with Romeo's servant Balthasar, and with Friar Laurence. The Prince of Verona and Lord and Lady Capulet soon arrive. When Lord Montague arrives, he brings the sad news that his wife (7) _____ earlier that evening. He says her death was caused by (8) _____ to Mantua.

Friar Laurence explains to the Prince of Verona and all assembled that he secretly married Romeo and Juliet on the day of Tybalt's death. He also admits he gave Juliet a sleeping potion that would give her a death-like appearance. The Friar says that he was there with Juliet when she awoke but left her alone in the tomb, where she took her own life. Paris' servant says that his master came to (9) _____ on Juliet's grave, and that he saw him (10) _____ on someone who was trying to enter Juliet's tomb. Balthasar, Romeo's servant, gives the Prince the letter he was supposed to deliver to Romeo's father. The Prince reads the letter and states that

As the play ends, Lord Capulet and Montague shake hands and offer their friendship to one another, with each of the men pledging to build beautiful (11) _____ to honor their memories. But the men both realize it was each family's (12) _____ that brought about the death of their children.

LAY FLOWERS	SEARCH THE GROUNDS	HATRED FOR THE OTHER
BALTHASAR	NOTIFY THE PRINCE	GRIEF OVER ROMEO'S EXILE
DRAW HIS SWORD	STABS HERSELF	BEGINNING TO AWAKEN
DIED	LEAVE THE VAULT	STATUES OF ROMEO AND JULIET

Shakespeare's
Romeo & Juliet

Tests for Acts 1-5,

including Essay Questions

NAME:_____   Act 1

In each of the three story-ordering sections below, put the items into the correct order, (1st, 2nd, 3rd, etc.), writing the numbers in the right column of each section.

Act 1, Scene 1

1) Benvolio learns that Romeo is sad because the woman he loves does not love him, and he advises Romeo to look at other women in order to help cure his sadness.	
2) Romeo, who did not take part in any of the fighting, has been very sad lately, but no one seems to know why. Furthermore, no one has seen him all day.	
3) As the play opens, another fight has erupted in the city of Verona between two warring families: the Capulets and the Montagues.	
4) The fighting between these two families stops only after the Prince of Verona issues a decree stating that whoever is caught fighting will be condemned to death.	
5) Romeo's parents are very concerned about him, and so they send his cousin Benvolio to try to find him.	

Act 1, Scenes 2 & 3

6) Juliet's father, Lord Capulet, speaks to a man who wants to marry Juliet, and he tells the young man that if he can win Juliet's heart, he will be in favor of the wedding.	
7) Juliet seems to have an open mind about the young man who wants to marry her, and she says she will see him at the gala feast and determine whether she likes him or not.	
8) In scene three, Juliet's mother learns that a young man wants to ask for Juliet's hand in marriage. She wants to know how Juliet feels about it.	
9) Lord Capulet then sends a servant on an errand, giving him a list of people to invite to the gala feast that will be held at the Capulet home.	
10) Unfortunately, the servant cannot read the guest list, but he meets Romeo and asks him for his help. Romeo discovers that the woman he loves will be at the gala feast.	

Act 1, Scenes 4 & 5

11) Romeo also tells Benvolio and Mercutio that he recently had a troubling dream of death.	
12) Once he is inside the Capulet home, Romeo looks for the woman he loves but sees Juliet instead, and it is love at first sight.	
13) When Romeo's enemy overhears him ask a servant about Juliet, he realizes they are enemies and immediately wants to have a duel to the death with Romeo.	
14) As Romeo walks to the gala feast with his cousin Benvolio and friend Mercutio, he tells them that he has a heavy heart and does not want to dance that evening.	
15) Before the trio enters the Capulet home to attend the gala feast, they put on masks to hide their faces since they were not invited.	

Name: _____   Act 1 (cont'd)

Identify the characters and families that were part of Act 1.
Use the list just below question #22 in order to make your choices.

16) Romeo is a member of this family.	
17) This person issued a decree that anyone in the city caught fighting would be condemned to death.	
18) This person is Romeo's cousin, and he is sent to find out what is wrong with Romeo.	
19) This woman is the object of Romeo's affection before he attends the gala event at the home of the Capulets.	
20) This young man is engaged to be married to Juliet.	
21) Juliet is a member of this family.	
22) This man overheard Romeo speak at the gala feast, and he knew Romeo was his enemy. He wanted to challenge Romeo to a duel right there during the gala feast.	

BENVOLIO	PARIS	TYBALT
THE PRINCE OF VERONA	ROSALINE	CAPULETS
MERCUTIO	MONTAGUES	JULIET

★★

Please provide the following answers in complete sentences. Please note each answer in this part counts as three answers, so check your sentences carefully after you write them.

23-25) What was the decree issued by the Prince of Verona?

26-28) In Scene 2, Paris speaks to Juliet's father. What does Paris want?

Name: _____   Act 1 (cont'd)

Please provide the following answers in complete sentences. Please note each answer in this part counts as three answers, so check your sentences carefully after you write them.

29-31) What does Romeo learn when he reads the guest list and finds out who has been invited to the Gala Feast?

32-34) What do you think Romeo's death dream tells about how the play will end?

35-37) How do Romeo's feelings toward Rosaline change during the Gala Feast?

38-40) How does Tybalt find out that Romeo, his enemy, is at the Gala Feast?

Note: For this test, each question is worth 2.5 points.

Act 1, Scene 1		Act 1, Scenes 2 & 3		Act 1, Scenes 4 & 5	
1)	5	6)	1	11)	2
2)	3	7)	5	12)	4
3)	1	8)	4	13)	5
4)	2	9)	2	14)	1
5)	4	10)	3	15)	3

16)	MONTAGUES
17)	THE PRINCE OF VERONA
18)	BENVOLIO
19)	ROSALINE
20)	PARIS
21)	CAPULETS
22)	TYBALT

23-25) What was the decree issued by the Prince of Verona?

THE PRINCE OF VERONA GREW TIRED OF SEEING THE FIGHTING GO ON BETWEEN THE TWO FAMILIES, AND HE DECREED THAT ANYONE CAUGHT FIGHTING IN THE STREETS WOULD BE CONDEMNED TO DEATH.

26-28) In Scene 2, Paris speaks to Juliet's father. What does Paris want?

PARIS WANTS TO MARRY JULIET, AND HE HAS COME TO SEE LORD CAPULET IN ORDER TO TALK TO HIM ABOUT A POSSIBLE MARRIAGE.

29-31) What does Romeo learn when he reads the guest list and finds out who has been invited to the Gala Feast?

ROMEO LEARNS THAT ROSALINE, THE WOMAN HE LOVES, WILL BE AT THE GALA FEAST.

32-34) What do you think Romeo's death dream tells about how the play will end?

STUDENT ANSWERS WILL VARY, BUT THEY SHOULD INDICATE AN UNDERSTANDING THAT ROMEO IS LIKELY TO DIE AT SOME POINT DURING THE PLAY, OR THAT THE PLAY WILL HAVE A SAD ENDING.

35-37) How do Romeo's feelings toward Rosaline change during the Gala Feast?

ROMEO LOOKED FOR ROSALINE, BUT DID NOT SEE HER AT THE FEAST. HOWEVER, ONCE ROMEO SAW JULIET, HE WAS NO LONGER IN LOVE WITH ROSALINE.

38-40) How does Tybalt find out that Romeo, his enemy, is at the Gala Feast?

WHEN ROMEO ASKS A SERVANT ABOUT JULIET, TYBALT OVERHEARS HIM, KNOWS INSTANTLY THAT THE VOICE IS THAT OF A MONTAGUE, AND ALSO RECOGNIZES THAT IT BELONGS TO ROMEO, HIS ENEMY.

NAME:_____ Act 2

Note: Follow directions *exactly* as they are written throughout this test.
Write your name at the top of each test page, using the lines provided.

In the story-ordering section below, put the items into the correct order,
(1st, 2nd, 3rd, etc.), writing the numbers in the right column of each section.

Act 2

1) Before the nurse gives Juliet the message from Romeo, she first asks Juliet if she has permission to leave the house and go to confession.	
2) In response to Juliet's pledge of love to him, Romeo promises that he will go and see Friar Laurence and ask the Friar to marry them.	
3) Romeo speaks to Juliet as she stands on the balcony outside of her bedroom, and they pledge their love to each other.	
4) Friar Laurence marries Romeo and Juliet in a secret ceremony.	
5) When the nurse comes to see Romeo, he tells her of the wedding plans.	
6) After making her pledge of love to Romeo, Juliet says that she will send a messenger to him at 9 o'clock the next morning to prove his love and honor.	
7) Friar Laurence tells Romeo he agrees to marry him to Juliet. The priest hopes their families will forget their hatred for each other so they can live in peace.	

****

8-11) WHO SAID WHAT? In the section below, write a name in the right hand column
to identify the person who made each of the statements listed in the left column.

What did he or she say?	Who said it?
8) This person expressed hope there could be peace between the two families because of the wedding.	
9) This person said that death could do whatever it wanted to do just as long as the wedding between Romeo and Juliet took place.	
10) This person complained about achy bones, pain, and being out of breath.	
11) This person wrote a letter to Romeo challenging him to a duel.	

Name: _____   Act 2 (cont'd)

12-17) Multiple Choice Questions	Directions: Underline the correct answer or answers.
12) What is the name of Romeo's sworn enemy?	A. Mercutio B. Tybalt C. Benvolio D. Paris
13) What is Romeo's family name?	A. Capulet B. Montague
14) What is Juliet's family name?	A. Capulet B. Montague
15-16) Who is Paris? (Choose two answers)	A. He is a Capulet B. He is a Montague C. He is a young man who wants to marry Juliet. D. He is a young relative of the Prince of Rome. E. He is a young relative of the Prince of Verona.
17) How would you describe what Juliet's parents know about her love for Romeo?	A. They are happy for her. B. They do not know anything about Juliet's love for Romeo. C. They are in favor of the wedding. D. They want to attend the wedding ceremony.

****

Please provide the following answers in complete sentences. Please note each answer in this part counts as two answers, so check your sentences carefully after you write them.

18-19) Describe how Juliet's nurse feels about being the messenger carrying the messages back and forth between the two lovers.

Name: _____   Act 2 (cont'd)

Please provide the following answers in complete sentences. Please note each answer in this part counts as two answers, so check your sentences carefully after you write them.

20-21) How do you think Romeo feels about the danger he faces in wanting to marry someone from a family that is his enemy?

| |
| |
| |
| |

22-23) Predict: How do you think Juliet's parents will react when they find out about her marriage to Romeo?

| |
| |
| |
| |

24-25) In what you have seen and read so far in the story of Romeo and Juliet, what has been the funniest or most interesting part?

| |
| |
| |
| |
| |

Did you follow the directions for this test exactly as they were written? If so, sign your name on the signature line below. Note: Credit will be given if you sign your name and it is determined that you *have,* in fact, correctly followed all directions given in this test.

Student Signature: _____

Note: For this test, each question is worth 4 points.

Story Ordering			
1)	6	5)	5
2)	3	6)	2
3)	1	7)	4
4)	7		

8-11) Who Said What?	
8) FRIAR LAURENCE	10) JULIET'S NURSE
9) ROMEO	11) TYBALT

12-17) Multiple Choice Questions
12) B. Tybalt
13) B. Montague
14) A. Capulet
15-16) **Note: There are two correct answers.**
C. He is a young man who wants to marry Juliet.
E. He is a young relative of the Prince of Verona.
17) B. They do not know about Juliet's love for Romeo.

18-19) Describe how Juliet's nurse feels about being the messenger carrying the messages back and forth between the two lovers.

SHE SEEMS TO FULLY ENJOY THE JOB, AND IS IN FAVOR OF THIS MATCH. SHE ALSO ENJOYS TEASING BOTH YOUNG LOVERS BY TALKING ABOUT OTHER THINGS BEFORE GETTING TO HER POINT.

20-21) How do you think Romeo feels about the danger he faces in wanting to marry someone from a family that is his enemy?

HE FEELS THAT AS LONG AS HE CAN MARRY JULIET, HE WILL FACE WHATEVER DANGER COMES HIS WAY.

22-23) Predict: How do you think Juliet's parents will react when they find out about her marriage to Romeo?

STUDENT ANSWERS WILL VARY. POSSIBLE ANSWERS INCLUDE: THEY WILL BE UPSET, THEY WILL TALK WITH THEIR DAUGHTER, THEY WILL TRY TO MAKE PEACE WITH ROMEO'S FAMILY, ETC.

24-25) In what you have seen and read so far in the story of Romeo and Juliet, what has been the funniest or most interesting part?

STUDENT ANSWERS WILL VARY.

Bonus Question (Note: The point value is to be determined by the instructor.)

FOR FULL CREDIT, THE STUDENT MUST WRITE HIS OR HER NAME ON THE TOP OF EACH OF THE THREE TEST PAGES, MUST UNDERLINE THE ANSWERS FOR QUESTIONS #12-16, MUST WRITE RESPONSES FOR #18-25 IN COMPLETE SENTENCES, AND MUST SIGN HIS OR HER NAME ON THE SIGNATURE LINE PROVIDED BELOW THE BONUS QUESTION.

Test for *Romeo & Juliet*

In each of the three story-ordering sections below, put the items into the correct order, (1st, 2nd, 3rd, etc.), writing the numbers in the right column of each section.

Act 3, Scene 1

1) Mercutio does not like hearing Tybalt taunt Romeo, so he challenges Tybalt to a duel. Romeo tries in vain to break up the fight, but Mercutio is killed.	
2) The Prince of Verona decrees that Romeo is to be banished from Verona forever.	
3) Benvolio tries to explain to the Prince of Verona just how the fighting happened.	
4) As Act Three begins, Tybalt is looking for Romeo. When he sees him, Tybalt taunts him and challenges him to a duel, but Romeo tries instead to be friendly in return.	
5) Romeo becomes angry at this and challenges Tybalt to a fight. Romeo slays Tybalt.	

Act 3, Scenes 2 & 3

6) We next see Friar Laurence telling Romeo that the Prince of Verona has banished him from the city.	
7) Juliet is beside herself with grief, for she has just learned from her nurse that Romeo has killed her cousin Tybalt.	
8) The Friar then tells Romeo to go and comfort his wife Juliet that night before fleeing to Mantua.	
9) Before the nurse leaves, Juliet gives her a ring to bring to Romeo.	
10) The nurse comforts Juliet by saying she knows Romeo is hiding in Friar Laurence's cell. The nurse also says she will go and tell Romeo to come to see Juliet that night.	

Act 3, Scenes 4 & 5

11) When Juliet's mother arrives, she speaks about the plans that have been made for Juliet to marry Paris. Juliet stuns her mother by saying she will marry Romeo.	
12) As a last resort, Juliet appeals to her nurse, but when even the nurse says she should	
13) Upon hearing her father's outburst of anger, Juliet begs her mother to delay the wedding ceremony, but her mother will not listen to her.	
14) As dawn approaches, Romeo and Juliet share one last kiss before he leaves for Mantua. The nurse arrives and tells Juliet that her mother will be up to see her.	
15) Next, when Lord Capulet enters Juliet's chamber and hears Juliet say she does not want to marry Paris, he explodes in anger and threatens to disown her.	

Name: _____   Act 3 (cont'd)

****

Mark each of these sentences as either true (T) or false (F).

16) Juliet's mother and father have known about her love for Romeo since the night Romeo and Juliet met.	
17) Juliet's nurse tells Juliet that the proposed marriage to Paris is a good thing.	
18) Juliet's father let her fully explain why she didn't want to marry Paris.	
19) Romeo fled from Juliet's bedroom at midnight so that he could get away safely.	
20) Juliet's mother will try to delay the wedding ceremony.	

21-30) Multiple Choice Questions	Directions: Underline the correct answer or answers.
I) What kinds of news and advice did Friar Laurence give to Romeo after Tybalt's death? (Choose all that apply.)	A. He said that the Prince's police officers would be looking for him. B. He said that Romeo should flee to Mantua. C. He said that Romeo should go and comfort Juliet. D. He told Romeo that Juliet thought he was a murderer. E. He told Romeo to act more like a man.
II) What happened when the nurse came to see Romeo in Friar Laurence's cell after the death of Tybalt? (Choose all that apply.)	A. She brought a ring from Juliet. B. She told Romeo she was very upset with him. C. She told Romeo that Juliet was weeping also. D. She told Romeo to act more like a man. E. She told Romeo to hurry and see Juliet that night.
III) How does Juliet surprise her mother when they speak about the plans for Juliet to marry Paris? (Choose all that apply.)	A. Juliet told her the plan for the wedding is too soon after Tybalt's death. B. Juliet told her she is too young to marry. C. Juliet told her mother that she will marry Romeo. D. Juliet told her of a bad dream she has had that has frightened her.
IV) What did Lord Capulet say when he expressed his anger with Juliet over her refusal to marry Paris? (Choose all that apply.)	A. Lord Capulet said his fist is ready to strike. B. Lord Capulet said that his only thought has been to find a marriage match for Juliet. C. Lord Capulet said he will go himself to see Friar Laurence. D. Lord Capulet said that he will not allow Juliet to live with him if she doesn't marry Paris.

Name: _____   Act 3 (cont'd)

Please provide the following answers in complete sentences. Please note each answer in this part counts as two answers, so check your sentences carefully after you write them.

31-32) Why do you think Romeo tried to be friendly towards Tybalt even after Tybalt challenged him to a duel?

33-34) Even though Romeo and Juliet are both very upset about Tybalt's death, what do you think is one thing that upsets them even more?

35-36) Do you think that Romeo will go to Mantua *with* Juliet or *without* her? Give one reason why you feel that way.

37-38) Do you think Juliet's father was right to be so angry with Juliet for refusing to agree to marry Paris?

39-40) What do you predict Friar Laurence will say to Juliet when he speaks to her?

Note: For this test, each question is worth 2.5 points.

Act 3, Scene 1		Act 3, Scenes 2 & 3		Act 3, Scenes 4 & 5	
1)	2	6)	4	11)	2
2)	5	7)	1	12)	5
3)	4	8)	5	13)	4
4)	1	9)	3	14)	1
5)	3	10)	2	15)	3

16)	F	21-30) Multiple Choice Questions	
17)	T	I)	**Note: This question has three answers.** 21) B. He said that Romeo should flee to Mantua. 22) C. He said that Romeo should go and comfort Juliet. 23) E. He told Romeo to act more like a man.
18)	F	II)	**Note: This question has three answers.** 24) A. She brought a ring from Juliet. 25) C. She told Romeo that Juliet was weeping also. 26) E. She told Romeo to hurry and see Juliet that night.
19)	F	III)	27) C. Juliet told her mother that she will marry Romeo.
20)	F	IV)	**Note: This question has three answers.** 28) A. Lord Capulet said his fist is ready to strike. 29) B. Lord Capulet said that his only thought has been to find a marriage match for Juliet. 30) D. Lord Capulet said that he will not allow Juliet to live with him if she doesn't marry Paris.

31-32) Why do you think Romeo tried to be friendly towards Tybalt even after Tybalt challenged him to a duel?

BECAUSE OF ROMEO'S MARRIAGE TO JULIET, TYBALT WAS NOW A RELATIVE OF ROMEO.

33-34) Even though Romeo and Juliet are both very upset about Tybalt's death, what do you think is one thing that upsets them even more?

STUDENT ANSWERS WILL VARY, BUT SHOULD INCLUDE THE IDEA THAT THEY WANT TO BE TOGETHER BUT CAN'T.

35-36) Do you think that Romeo will go to Mantua *with* Juliet or *without* her? Give one reason why you feel that way.

STUDENT ANSWERS WILL VARY.

37-38) Do you think Juliet's father was right to be so angry with Juliet for refusing to agree to marry Paris?

STUDENT ANSWERS WILL VARY.

39-40) What do you predict Friar Laurence will say to Juliet when he speaks to her?

STUDENT ANSWERS WILL VARY.

NAME:_____   Act 4

In each of the story-ordering sections below, put the items into the correct order, (1st, 2nd, 3rd, etc.), writing the numbers in the right column of each section.

Act 4, Scenes 1, 2 & 3

1) When Juliet is alone in her chamber, she begins to go mad and imagines that she sees Tybalt's ghost trying to find and kill Romeo.	
2) When Juliet goes to Friar Laurence cell, she finds Paris there. They are unfriendly to one another. The Friar asks Paris to leave, as he wants to speak to Juliet alone.	
3) Immediately after Juliet drinks the sleeping potion, she falls back upon her bed.	
4) The priest tells Juliet of a plan to drink a sleeping potion the night before her wedding to Paris is to occur. Juliet takes the potion and returns to her home.	
5) Once Juliet is alone with Friar Laurence, she asks for his help and tells him that if he will not help her, she will take her own life.	

Act 4, Scenes 4 & 5

6) The nurse is the first to discover that Juliet appears to be dead. Soon afterwards, Juliet's parents learn of the "death" of their daughter.	
7) Friar Laurence offers words of comfort to Juliet's parents, to Paris, and to the nurse.	
8) The priest then suggests that everyone follow Juliet's body as it is carried to the grave.	
9) Next, Friar Laurence and Paris arrive, ready to take Juliet to the church for the wedding ceremony. Juliet's father breaks the sad news to Paris of Juliet's "death."	
10) Juliet's mother and father have already been awake that morning for many hours preparing for the wedding feast. They do not yet know what has happened to Juliet.	

11-13) What were three things that Juliet feared might happen if she drank the potion that Friar Laurence gave to her?

11)

12)

13)

Name: _____   Act 4 (cont'd)

14-21) Multiple Choice Questions	Directions: Underline the correct answer or answers.
I) How did Paris act towards Juliet when they met in Friar Laurence's cell? (Choose all that apply)	A. He was very kind to Juliet. B. He acted as if he owned her as his wife. C. He acted as if he knew she was in love with Romeo. D. He spoke to her as if she were just a young girl.
II) How did Lord Capulet act towards his daughter after Juliet came back from Friar Laurence's cell? (Choose all that apply)	A. He was still very angry with her because of her disobedience and disrespect. B. He wanted nothing to do with her because of how she had acted earlier. C. He was pleased that Juliet was now saying she would go ahead with the plans to marry Paris. D. He did not have any reaction to her at all.
III) What was happening at the home of the Capulets on the morning of Juliet's wedding? (Choose all that apply)	A. Paris arrived with some musicians. B. The nurse worked to get Juliet's clothes ready. C. Lord and Lady Capulet prepared for the wedding. D. Servants brought supplies for the wedding feast. E. Juliet cried herself to sleep up in her bedroom chamber.
IV) What did Juliet's father do after he found out that his daughter was "dead"? (Choose all that apply)	A. He wept over the "death" of his daughter. B. He told servants to go and tell the Prince of Verona about Juliet's "death." C. He told Paris the sad news of Juliet's "death." D. He told the servants that all of the things prepared for Juliet's wedding would now be used for her funeral. E. He told the nurse that Juliet's "death" was her fault.

Name: _____   Act 4 (cont'd)

Please provide the following answers in complete sentences. Be sure to check your sentences carefully after you write them.

22) Do you think Paris treated Juliet fairly when he met her in Friar Laurence's cell?

23) Do you think Juliet should have acted differently or spoken in a different way when she talked to Paris in Friar Laurence's cell?

24) How do you think Friar Laurence felt as he stood with Juliet's family after she was found to be "dead"?

25) What do you predict will happen when Juliet wakes up from her "death"?

Note: For this test, each question is worth 4 points.

Act 4, Scenes 1, 2 & 3		Act 4, Scenes 4 & 5	
1)	4	6)	2
2)	1	7)	4
3)	5	8)	5
4)	3	9)	3
5)	2	10)	1

11-13) What were three things that Juliet feared might happen if she drank the potion that Friar Laurence gave to her? (Note: Accept answers in any order.)	
11)	IT MIGHT NOT WORK.
12)	IT MIGHT KILL HER.
13)	SHE MIGHT BE BURIED ALIVE IN THE VAULT BEFORE ROMEO ARRIVED TO SAVE HER.

14-21) Multiple Choice Questions	
I)	14) B. He acted as if he owned her as his wife.
II)	15) C. He was pleased that Juliet was now saying she would go ahead with the plans to marry Paris.
III)	**Note: This question has three answers.** 16) A. Paris arrived with some musicians. 17) C. Lord and Lady Capulet prepared for the wedding. 18) D. Servants brought supplies for the wedding feast.
IV)	**Note: This question has three answers.** 19) A. He wept over the "death" of his daughter. 20) C. He told Paris the sad news of Juliet's "death." 21) D. He told the servants that all of the things prepared for Juliet's wedding would now be used for her funeral.

22) Do you think Paris treated Juliet fairly when he met her in Friar Laurence's cell?

STUDENT ANSWERS WILL VARY.

23) Do you think Juliet should have acted differently or spoken in a different way when she talked to Paris in Friar Laurence's cell?

STUDENT ANSWERS WILL VARY.

24) How do you think Friar Laurence felt as he stood with Juliet's family after she was found to be "dead"?

STUDENT ANSWERS WILL VARY BUT SHOULD INDICATE IN SOME WAY THAT FRIAR LAURENCE WAS BEING DISINGENUOUS.

25) What do you predict will happen when Juliet wakes up from her "death"?

STUDENT ANSWERS WILL VARY, AND COULD DEPEND ON WHETHER OR NOT THEY HAVE PREVIOUS KNOWLEDGE ABOUT THE STORY'S ENDING.

Test for *Romeo & Juliet*

Note: Follow directions *exactly* as they are written throughout this test.
Write your name at the top of each test page, using the lines provided.

In each of the three story-ordering sections below, put the items into the correct order,
(1st, 2nd, 3rd, etc.), writing the numbers in the right column of each section.

Act 5, Scenes 1 & 2

1) As a result, the Friar realizes he must hurry to Juliet's side to be with her when she awakens from her sleep. He also fears Romeo will think that Juliet is really dead.	
2) As the final act opens, we see Romeo thinking about a dream he had concerning Juliet. In the dream he died, but Juliet brought him back to life with her kisses.	
3) Romeo is distraught about the news of Juliet's death and goes to an apothecary to buy poison so that he can take his own life.	
4) Romeo's sweet thoughts are interrupted when his servant arrives and tells him that Juliet is dead, and that her body lies in the Capulet family tomb in Verona.	
5) In the next scene, Friar Laurence discovers that a letter he wrote to Romeo did not get delivered. The letter described the plan to give Juliet a sleeping potion.	

Act 5, Scene 3, Part A

6) Paris' servant soon whistles. Romeo has arrived, along with his servant Balthasar. Romeo instructs Balthasar to take a letter to his father, and leave him alone.	
7) Once he is alone, Romeo starts to pry open Juliet's tomb, but Paris confronts him and tries to arrest him. They duel and Romeo stabs Paris, mortally wounding him.	
8) In an act of desperation inside the tomb, Romeo speaks to Juliet and embraces her. He then drinks the poison he has brought and dies.	
9) In the last moment of his life, Paris asks Romeo to grant him one request. He asks that his body be placed in the tomb beside that of Juliet. Romeo honors this request.	
10) Paris arrives at the graveyard where Juliet is buried. He tells his servant to whistle if he sees anyone else enter.	

Act 5, Scene 3, Part B

11) In the scene that follows the discovery of the bodies of Romeo and Juliet, Friar Laurence tells the Prince of Verona that he secretly married the couple.	
12) Upon hearing this news, Juliet orders Friar Laurence to leave the burial chamber. Once she is alone, Juliet takes her own life, stabbing herself with Romeo's dagger.	
13) When Friar Laurence enters the tomb, he sees not only the dead bodies of Romeo and Paris, but he also sees that Juliet is starting to awaken from her sleep.	
14) The fathers of Romeo and Juliet realize that the hatred between their families brought about the death of their children.	
15) After she awakens, Juliet asks Friar Laurence about her husband Romeo. The Friar has to break the sad news to her that Romeo is dead.	

Multiple Choice Questions	Directions: Underline the one correct answer for each question.
16) In Romeo's dream, what did he become after Juliet brought him back to life with her kisses?	A. A man liked by the Capulets B. A prince C. A king D. A rich man
17) What did Romeo give to the druggist in exchange for the poison he purchased?	A. Silver B. Gold C. Copper D. Bronze
18) Why didn't Friar Laurence's friend Friar John deliver the letter to Romeo?	A. He said he was not going to the city of Mantua. B. He was detained inside a house in the city of Verona and could not go to Mantua. C. He could not find Romeo's servant Balthasar. D. He could not find Romeo's house in Mantua.
19) Why did Paris confront Romeo in the courtyard outside of Juliet's tomb?	A. He was jealous of Romeo's love for Juliet. B. He thought Romeo was going to dishonor the graves of Juliet and Tybalt. C. Paris and Romeo were enemies. D. He wanted to kill Romeo.
20) What is the one fact that Friar Laurence did *not* tell the Prince of Verona about the bloody murder scene?	A. That he was with Juliet when she awoke from her death-like sleep. B. That Juliet killed herself with Romeo's dagger. C. That Paris came to lay flowers on Juliet's grave. D. That the Friar said he gave Juliet the sleeping potion that put Juliet into the death-like sleep.

Name: _____   Act 5 (cont'd)

Please provide the following answers in complete sentences.
Be sure to check your sentences carefully after you write them.

21) Describe the change in Romeo's mood from the time he thought of the dream he had of Juliet to the time that Balthasar told him Juliet was dead.

22) What is the danger that Friar Laurence sensed when he found out that Romeo did not receive the letter that had been sent to him?

23) Did Paris know that Romeo was in love with Juliet? Explain your answer.

24) Do you think Balthasar did the right thing by disobeying Romeo's order and not delivering the letter to Romeo's father? Explain your answer.

25) How would you describe the mood of Lord Capulet as he offered a hand of friendship to Lord Montague?

Bonus Question

Did you follow the directions for this test exactly as they were written? If so, sign your name on the signature line below. **Note:** Credit will be given if you sign your name and it is determined that you *have*, in fact, correctly followed all directions given in this test.

Student Signature: _____

Note: For this test, each question is worth 4 points.

Act 5, Scenes 1 & 2		Act 5, Scene 3, Part A		Act 1, Scene 3, Part B	
1)	5	6)	2	11)	4
2)	1	7)	3	12)	3
3)	3	8)	5	13)	1
4)	2	9)	4	14)	5
5)	4	10)	1	15)	2

16)	C	17)	B	18)	B	19)	B	20)	C

21) Describe the change in Romeo's mood from the time he thought of the dream he had of Juliet to the time that Balthasar told him Juliet was dead.

HIS MOOD WENT FROM ELATION TO UTTER DESPAIR.

22) What is the danger that Friar Laurence sensed when he found out that Romeo did not receive the letter that had been sent to him?

HE KNEW THAT JULIET WOULD WAKE UP IN THE TOMB ALL ALONE.

23) Did Paris know that Romeo was in love with Juliet? Explain your answer.

STUDENT ANSWERS CAN VARY FROM INDICATING THAT PARIS HAD NO KNOWLEDGE OF ROMEO'S LOVE FOR JULIET, TO A STATEMENT THAT HE MIGHT HAVE HAD SOME SUSPICIONS ABOUT IT.

24) Do you think Balthasar did the right thing by disobeying Romeo's order and not delivering the letter to Romeo's father? Explain your answer.

STUDENT ANSWERS WILL VARY. THEY MAY INCLUDE THE STATEMENT THAT HE WANTED TO GIVE THE LETTER TO THE PRINCE OF VERONA.

25) How would you describe the mood of Lord Capulet as he offered a hand of friendship to Lord Montague?

STUDENT ANSWERS WILL VARY, BUT SHOULD INCLUDE SOME MENTION OF THE IDEA THAT THE HATRED BETWEEN THE TWO FAMILIES WAS A FACTOR IN THE DEATH OF ROMEO AND JULIET.

Bonus Question (Note: The point value is to be determined by the instructor.)

FOR FULL CREDIT, THE STUDENT MUST WRITE HIS OR HER NAME ON THE TOP OF EACH OF THE THREE TEST PAGES, MUST UNDERLINE THE ANSWERS FOR QUESTIONS #16-20, MUST WRITE RESPONSES FOR #21-25 IN COMPLETE SENTENCES, AND MUST SIGN HIS OR HER NAME ON THE SIGNATURE LINE PROVIDED BELOW THE BONUS QUESTION.

Essay Question for *Romeo & Juliet*

NAME:_____   Essay #1

Write an essay in which you discuss how *Romeo & Juliet* is related to the quotation that is shown in the box below. In your essay, (1) describe what you think the statement below means, (2) state whether you agree or disagree that it applies to *Romeo & Juliet*, and (3) provide reasons to support your opinion.

"Speak of me as I am... (as) one that loved not wisely but too well."
                                                    -Shakespeare, *Othello*, Act 5, Scene 2

Essay Question for *Romeo & Juliet*

NAME:_____   Essay #2

The story of *Romeo & Juliet* ends tragically with both of the young lovers committing suicide. There were many adults involved in their lives, and many of those adults were either opposed to the romance between Romeo and Juliet, or they took action in some way that might have been at least partly responsible for the deaths of the two young lovers. What actions do you think the adults in *Romeo & Juliet* could or should have taken in order to prevent the tragic deaths of the young couple?

Appendix B

The ***Romeo & Juliet Story Summary Worksheets & Tests*** will help students meet the Common Core Standards for Reading and Writing that are listed below:

READING: Key Ideas and Details
1. Cite strong and thorough textual evidence to support analysis of what the text says explicitly as well as inferences drawn from the text.
2. Determine a theme or central idea of a text and analyze in detail its development over the course of the text, including how it emerges and is shaped and refined by specific details; provide an objective summary of the text.
3. Analyze how complex characters (e.g., those with multiple or conflicting motivations) develop over the course of a text, interact with other characters, and advance the plot or develop the theme.

READING: Craft and Structure
6. Analyze a particular point of view or cultural experience reflected in a work of literature from outside the United States, drawing on a wide reading of world literature.

READING: Range of Reading and Level of Text Complexity
10. By the end of grade 9, read and comprehend literature, including stories, dramas, and poems, in the grades 9–10 text complexity band proficiently, with scaffolding as needed at the high end of the range.

WRITING: Text types and Purposes
1. Write arguments to support claims in an analysis of substantive topics or texts, using valid reasoning and relevant and sufficient evidence.
1d. Establish and maintain a formal style and objective tone while attending to the norms and conventions of the discipline in which they are writing.
3c. Use a variety of techniques to sequence events so that they build on one another to create a coherent whole.

WRITING: Production and Distribution of Writing
4. Produce clear and coherent writing in which the development, organization, and style are appropriate to task, purpose, and audience.

WRITING: Research to Build and Present Knowledge
9. Draw evidence from literary or informational texts to support analysis, reflection, and research.

WRITING: Range of Writing
10. Write routinely over extended time frames (time for research, reflection, and revision) and shorter time frames (a single sitting or a day or two) for a range of tasks, purposes, and audiences.

Sources:
http://www.corestandards.org/assets/CCSSI_ELA%20Standards.pdf

http://www.p12.nysed.gov/ciai/common_core_standards/pdfdocs/p12_common_core_learning_standards_ela.pdf

About the Author

Gary Ciesla is a prolific writer and a veteran Special Education teacher who has worked in a variety of interesting and challenging classroom environments. He has taught in state and federal prisons, in institutions for troubled youth, in a program for autistic children with Asperger's Syndrome, in an Alternative Education program, and most recently, at EF International in Tarrytown, New York, where he first taught English to students from around the world, and then managed the EF/NY University Pathways Program.

As an author, Mr. Ciesla has written and published *The Little Book of Secret Code Puzzles: Pearls of Wisdom & Encouragement Waiting to be Discovered, Shakespeare's Macbeth: Story Summary Worksheets and Tests,* and *The Logic Puzzle Project.* He lives in Highland Falls, New York.

If you wish to contact Mr. Ciesla, he can be reached, via email, at the following address: *gary.ciesla@gmail.com.*